THE FAST PATH

Adventures in Meditation & Spirituality

By Shiva – Tony Chester

The Fast Path

Adventures in Meditation & Spirituality
By Shiva – Tony Chester

Published by
Mystic-Buddha Publishing House, LLC
San Antonio, Texas

First Edition
Printed in the United States of America

Library of Congress Control Number: 2008936219
ISBN-13   978-0-9820505-0-7
ISBN-10   0-9820505-0-X

THIS BOOK IS LOVINGLY DEDICATED TO
MY TEACHER, RAMA

HIS LIGHT AND ENERGY ALONG WITH HIS
PROFOUND GUIDANCE AWAKENED US TO THE
ENLIGHTENMENT PROCESS

Table of Contents

Introduction

I am humbled and awed that I was able to study with one of the most powerful and loving spiritual teachers of modern times. His teachings did not just guide, but pushed me at amazing speeds down the path towards enlightenment. This speed of change in my life sometimes left me confused and a little dazed at first. But each teaching cleared and lifted my spirit in the end.

As I reflect back on the story of my "white water" trip towards enlightenment, I see that my story is really a series of smaller stories—a series of impactful moments. I would like to share with you now these stories of my trip down *The Fast Path*.

Chapter One – Preparation

Mickey

It was 1979. Mickey and I sat out in the open air in what used to be the cab of his "Frogmobile." The Frogmobile was an old green 1963 Ford pickup that had been rolled. The cab had been crushed in the accident, so my friend Mickey had chopped off the roof. The results were perfect for rabbit hunting or just sitting out in the open enjoying the view! We were parked on a deserted dirt road overlooking Las Cruces, New Mexico. This was a place we had come to many times when we were students at New Mexico State. Now, years later, we were once again sipping some cold beer and enjoying the warm New Mexico night.

"Have you ever been drawn to a place?" I queried.

"No, not that I know of. What do you mean?" Mickey asked.

"Ever since I was a child, I've been pulled like a magnet to the West Coast. I don't really know why. It's just kind of a longing."

"No, can't say as I have ever felt that way," he responded.

We sat in silence for a long time. Mickey was that type of friend. We really didn't have to talk to enjoy each other's company. The lights of Las Cruces looked like a small jewel box below a vast canopy of stars. It was so beautiful!

As a cool breeze from the west blew through the sagebrush and gently caressed my face, Mickey mentioned that he had heard about this fellow in California who could disappear and levitate.

"This guy is supposed to perform all kinds of miracles. They say he can glow, cause things to disappear — all sorts of things," he said.

I looked across the bench seat. "Really? You think that this guy actually does that?"

"I don't know, but I heard that he does.

"What is he, some sort of Indian Yogi?" I wondered out loud.

"No. He is supposed to be an American but he does have this strange spiritual name of Atmananda."

"I'd like to see this guy sometime," I mused.

We sat in silence for a few more minutes and then I opened a couple more beers and moved on to a different subject. Soon thoughts of Atmananda were lost in the haze that engulfed my consciousness during this time of my life.

Elizabeth

"Tony, if you don't have any plans for lunch today, could I join you?"

I recognized the voice. It was Elizabeth, the executive secretary from upstairs.

It was 1980; I was the Supervisor of Administrative Services at the United Church of Religious Science Headquarters in Los Angeles. I was working my way through the U.C.R.S. School of Ministry and only a couple of months from graduating.

I was taken aback by Elizabeth's request. I really didn't know her that well, but something in her voice told me that this was a serious matter, not a social thing.

"You've picked a good time; I have no lunch plans," I said. "How about 11:45, if that's okay?"

She agreed.

The Headquarters lunchroom had a couple of picnic tables set up in the patio for an outdoor eating area. I cleared the leaves off one of the small tables and chairs and I sat down and waited. It was a sunny and cool winter day in Los Angeles.

Soon I saw her blond hair. She was an attractive woman, slightly older than I was. She always dressed impeccably and had a light air about her. She was, by far, the best secretary in the building.

Today, however, she seemed a bit nervous as she worked her way across the lunchroom towards the patio.

"I really didn't know if I should confide in you, but you are going to be a minister soon and I have come to trust your judgment," she said as she sat down.

I was flattered, and yet I knew that I had not finished the second year of counseling at school. I hoped that I was up to the situation.

"I have met this spiritual teacher called Atmananda," she said.

Something rang familiar, but I did not make the connection to my conversation with Mickey from a year before.

"I feel very excited about studying with him, but he is so powerful and I am concerned as to whether or not it is a good idea. In the past, I have lost myself in men and organizations. I just need a second opinion concerning this matter," she explained.

I was highly skeptical of any "Gurus." I was, however, somewhat curious and I asked her to tell me about him.

As she talked, her face became very animated and her whole being seemed to light up as she described her experiences with her teacher. I could see that she was experiencing a true spiritual awakening. Something within me stirred and I knew that this was "right" for her.

Finally, the lunch hour was almost over and she looked at me, waiting for my advice.

"I don't agree with the whole concept of having a 'Guru.' There are so many out there that take advantage of spiritual seekers. I am a firm believer in self-reliance," I began. "However, I can see that in this case, it appears to be a wonderful experience for you. I think you should continue studying with him. Just question and test all of his recommendations and see if they apply to you."

She smiled and said, "That's exactly what he said!"

She seemed at ease now and as we stood to leave, she looked at me and tilted her head.

"Would you like to attend one of our meetings? There is an open meditation this weekend."

The possibility shook me up. I had the feeling that if I did, I would not continue the course I had charted for my life. After all, I was married with children and going to graduate soon to become a minister. I was unwilling to change my direction. I must admit that I was also a little afraid and, quite honestly, not yet ready to drop everything. Therefore, I declined.

The Poster

The Sunday congregation had just finished singing "Oh What a Beautiful Morning!" and it was time for the announcements. I stood up behind the podium.

"I have decided that the first spiritual excursion in our Self-Discovery Outings will be..."

It was 1982 and I was now thirty-six years old. Everything in my life had just fallen apart. I had recently lost my position as the minister of the Beverly Hills Science of Mind Center (a New Age metaphysical church), and was in the midst of a divorce.

It was a tough time of transition and I was attempting to regain some of my purpose and self-esteem by creating another New Thought Church in Marina Del Rey, California.

This new church, "The L.I.F.E. Center," had around twenty people as a core group.

Shawn had come up with the idea of naming it the L.I.F.E. Center. It was an acronym for "Living in Full Expression." Shawn was one of my assistant ministers. She was a beautiful, vivacious redhead and her enthusiasm was impossible to constrain. The name and concept was so wonderful that it was immediately adopted.

Some of the younger crowd from Beverly Hills had followed me to this new church and there seemed to be a lot of excitement and energy in this new endeavor. We worked as a group of friends trying to create a caring spiritual community.

As part of our commitment to L.I.F.E., we decided to have a monthly Self-Discovery Outing as a group social activity. All of us began looking for some interesting activities for these outings and we kicked around a number of great options.

On this particular Sunday morning, I had bought an L.A. Times. I didn't usually read a paper before church. However, today was different. I opened the paper to see a full-page color advertisement of this strange meditation teacher called Atmananda.

My mind went back to Mickey and Elizabeth. For the first time I made the connection.

The sheer energy of the poster captivated me. It was really quite extraordinary and its power fascinated me. In addition to his picture, Atmananda listed his past lives as a teacher complete with locations and dates. I felt intuitively that this strange spiritual resume was, in fact, true! I was hooked.

I showed the poster to Shawn and she became immediately excited. Right then and there, it was decided to make this our first outing.

Now, here I stood in front of my small congregation. As I held up this poster for everyone to see, there was a gasp let out by the congregation. Everyone shifted in their seats. Some seemed truly excited while others were clearly uncomfortable. Their reaction to the energy of the poster both surprised and impressed me as I announced that our Self-Discovery Outing would be attending a public meditation with this teacher called Atmananda.

I had a gut feeling that this would be a most interesting outing.

Chapter 2 – The First Four-Night Seminar

Self-Discovery Outing

On the night of our Self-Discovery Outing with Atmananda, my group gathered in front of the Sheraton Miramar Hotel in Santa Monica. Shawn had everyone wearing our L.I.F.E. Center sweatshirts and we each had notebooks to record our experiences. In this way, we planned to draw from successful presentations and incorporate them into our future activities.

I noticed that a long line of people had formed outside the hotel.

"Wonderful!" I thought sarcastically. "There must be some sort of political convention being held here. We will have to wade through all of these people to find out where this seminar is being held."

After inquiring, I was surprised to find that all of these people were also here to attend this meditation. I had no idea that so many people were interested in meditation! We then waited in line and finally made our way into the large meeting room.

I was, once again, astonished at what I saw.

There were about fourteen hundred people. The size of the crowd shocked me. I was also astounded at the quality of spiritual aspirants that were there. All of them seemed so clean and, well, for lack of a better word, pure.

While we registered, I was handed some high quality brochures and a funny little button that said, "Know Thyselves."

I told my friends to pay close attention and to take notes. This fellow was obviously doing something right and I wanted to model my future seminars after him.

About that time, Atmananda entered the room surrounded by four bodyguards. I found it odd that he would need security.

We scurried to find a seat as Atmananda sat down and said, "Good evening." He seemed so at ease and friendly as he announced that we were going to meditate to some music by a musical group called Tangerine Dream.

As the music was turned on and the lights dimmed, I felt a subtle but extremely powerful rush of energy. Then the lights in the room started to change. I wondered how he managed to create this wonderful golden glow and have everyone in front of me be outlined in this white light. I could not figure it out! Then I realized that I was actually seeing an aura!

I was thirty-six years old and although I had attended scores of self-discovery seminars and meditation retreats, I had never experienced seeing an aura. I had had friends who could see auras and I myself had read books about them, but I had long since resigned myself to be one of those people who would never see one. I was absolutely blown away. And the energy! It just kept getting stronger and stronger! Words fail me when I start to describe how it was to meditate with him. Waves of energy flowed up my spine. My body was rigid and various parts of my being lit up inside as the meditation energy increased. My thoughts stopped and my mind was clear. I was intensely aware of my surroundings, and yet I did not feel the need to analyze or think about it. I was in a wonderful space — meditation at last! Incredible seems a gross understatement!

At the end of the evening, my group left in a dazed and startled awareness. As we walked outside, everything looked clear and clean, like after a spring rain. I felt energized and astounded by what I had just experienced. I knew that I had to return the next night, no matter what.

Shawn's Boyfriend

On the second night of meditation, I arranged to carpool with Shawn and her boyfriend. Shawn had been dating this psychic, and she was so excited from her first night with Atmananda that she insisted that he come along.

They picked me up in his car and I felt a little apprehensive about going with them. I almost drove my own car, but Shawn and her boyfriend soon talked me out of it.

We arrived, registered and entered as the night before. Once again, the energy went through the roof and the room started to turn gold!

I found out that the phenomenon of experiencing the room turning gold happens when Enlightenment is made manifest in the room. It is usually the result of a teacher going into a state of "Samadhi." [1] The teacher dissolves into the Light of Eternity and there is nothing left but the doorway that he has gone through. This doorway then fills the room with eternal light.

I noticed that Shawn's boyfriend was becoming more and more agitated as the meditation progressed.

Finally, the meditation ended and Atmananda asked if there were any questions. Someone asked about women and Enlightenment.

As Atmananda started to speak, Shawn's boyfriend grabbed her arm and said, "I've seen enough! This guy is a fake! Let's go!"

I started to say that I wanted to stay, but he was already dragging her toward the exit.

---

[1] Samadhi is a Hindu and Buddhist technical term that usually denotes higher levels of concentrated meditation, and is considered a precursor for enlightenment, or Nirvana, in Buddhism.

Having no way home, I too stood up and left. As we walked out, I heard Atmananda say, "Now there is a good example of why some women don't attain Enlightenment!"

We left among the giggles, scrutiny, and scorn of over fourteen hundred people.

As we rode through Hollywood to my apartment, I quietly sat in the back and endured Shawn's boyfriend going through all kinds of rationalizations and ego rebellion. I was disgusted at his constant ranting and raving as he angrily trashed Atmananda.

I resolved that I would not place myself in this predicament again. I felt terrible at having to leave the meditation early because of this jerk. I felt cheated and embarrassed by the rude display of ego by this man who obviously lacked humility.

Taking the Step

The following night I declined the invitation to ride with some of my other friends and I took my own car. I did not even sit with anyone I knew. I had a wonderful time! When Atmananda said that he would be accepting students the following evening, I decided to apply as a student to this wonderful being.

After the meeting I caught up with Shawn, or rather I should say she caught up with me.

"I'm so sorry about last night," she said. "My friend was horrible."

"So how is he?" I asked.

"I dumped him," she grinned. "I couldn't be around such an asshole."

I grinned and laughed.

"I hope you don't mind, but I decided to apply as a student. I still plan to be active in our church. It's just something I feel I should do," Shawn said.

I looked into her eyes and grinned. "You have taken the words right out of my mouth," I said.

On the fourth night, I waited with great anticipation as the evening ended. After everyone left, those of us who had applied moved to the front of the room. Atmananda looked at us one by one; some he accepted and others he said needed to clear up something in their life. When he got to me, I felt my soul being examined. He smiled and accepted me! I felt such joy! I had finally come home.

Shawn and I, along with two others from the L.I.F.E. Center, became students that night.

The strange pull to the West Coast also ended that night.

The Fast Path

Chapter 3 – Center Meetings

My First Student Meeting

I stood outside the Unity By The Sea Church in Santa Monica. The air was cool and I could smell the sea breeze. This is the place where the student meetings were being held. I noticed a line of people standing outside the building. Everyone was happy and excited. I joined them and soon found myself walking into a completely new chapter in my life.

As I entered through the doors, I was a little nervous and felt awkward as I walked into the greeting area where I was registered. I was then ushered into the large sanctuary.

The main hall was supposed to hold over six hundred people and it was full. I sat and listened to the strange but wonderful electronic music and felt waves of energy flow through the room. The crowd would start to murmur and talk softly, a wave of energy would flow through the room and everyone would be quiet, and then slowly the murmuring would resume and increase again until the next wave when everything would be quiet again.

Finally, Atmananda walked into the room and the energy rose to startling heights. We meditated to Tangerine Dream and I was absolutely blown away.

At the end of the meditation he stated, "Looks like the Tibetans are finally arriving." People laughed.

I had no idea what he was talking about. I did not see any Tibetans. Then I noticed some of the students were looking at me. Now I was confused.

He talked briefly about a desert trip he and a few of the students had just returned from after the public meditation. He asked one of the students to relate what had happened out in the desert. There was a gasp from the students in the front. However, I could not quite hear enough to understand.

Then he looked at us and said, "For those of you that didn't hear what was just said, my name is no longer Atmananda; I am Rama."

The room turned gold and I do not remember much of what followed. I do have a clear sensation that whatever it was must have been incredible.

The following days I discovered that it was extremely easy to set up a meditation routine, and my meditations really took off! I had meditated before using techniques I had picked up in Transcendental Meditation, a few meditation seminars at Zen Centers, and a variety of other spiritual workshops and seminars. But, until now, sitting down to meditate had always been a chore. I had never been able to manage any consistency much less be able to stop my thoughts. Suddenly it was easy and powerful.

I started to change in new and magnificent ways. I resigned my ministerial position at the L.I.F.E. Center. It just did not seem right for me anymore. As I left, I installed Shawn to take it over. Even though she was now a student of Rama, she still liked being a part of the L.I.F.E. Center. Shawn was perfect for this new role.

I was now a student, and I was headed in a whole new direction.

Don't Trash

After being a student for over a month, I came to realize that every meeting was an unpredictable event. The structure was centered on Rama and meditation. I began to understand that he, of all the people I had ever met, was the most unpredictable. He was also the most powerful and enlightened being I had run across.

On this evening, I was sitting as usual, close to the front, and enjoying the waves of energy that always happened before each meeting.

Suddenly Rama came into the room. He was obviously upset. He sat down, turned off the music and glared out into the body of students. The room turned golden and my spine started to straighten on its own.

"I have observed that many of you are trashing me!" he said. "The karma is too intense for trashing your teacher! It is impossible to see completely why I do and say the things I do. You simply cannot see with the depth needed to understand what I do!"

"This being so, it is in your best interest to just come and meditate and not pass judgment on me or try to expect me to live up or down to your unenlightened and limited expectations!"

The silence was astounding. The energy in the room was electric. It was clear that he had struck a nerve. I wondered at how he could speak with such force and apparent anger and the room remained this intense golden color!

The following week he was once again on the same topic.

"I can't believe some of you! Now you are trashing other spiritual teachers!" he exclaimed.

"Who are you to pass judgment on any spiritual teacher? Who sat you up on the judgment seat and gave you authority to say that this teacher is right or this teacher is not! You think that you are so advanced that you are above the karma of your deeds and actions," he said.

"Let me tell you! You don't know the first thing as to why these beautiful individuals are doing what they are doing. You have not bothered to look deeply into the people that they have to work with. If you had, you would have a kinder, gentler assessment of them and their place in Eternity!"

"Just as it is extremely bad karma to trash me, it is equally bad karma to trash any spiritual teacher. Don't do it! If you cannot speak with respect, then don't speak at all!"

Once again, the room was stunned. How did he know that I had been discussing some of the television evangelists this week and had really trashed them? I resolved not to do that again.

The third week we were expecting Rama to come again in a serious mood. He did not disappoint us.

What must I do to instill any sense of etiquette in you people?" he exclaimed in disgust.

"Now you are trashing fellow spiritual aspirants, your fellow students! I just cannot believe how mean and vicious you are with each other! Don't you see that every one of these beautiful souls in here is trying to attain Enlightenment and that makes them pretty special. Just because they do not dress the way you think they should, or maybe they haven't yet read the books or know the jargon that you know, doesn't give you the right to speak of them in a condescending way. If you are so advanced that you can pass judgment on anyone in this room, then you are obviously far too advanced for this study and you should leave right now!"

The room was totally still. His point had been made.

Okay, I thought. Do not trash my teacher. Do not trash any spiritual teacher. Do not trash any spiritual aspirants. Got it!

The next week Rama walked in, turned down the music and quietly said, "Everyone and everything is your spiritual teacher. Don't trash your teachers."

As I meditated and journaled these meetings, I came to some rather interesting insights. I realized that the habit of "trashing" someone or something alleviated me of the responsibility of looking at that person's point of view. As long as

I could make someone wrong or misguided, then I would not have to look at myself.

I also observed that after the first week a few students left. They figured that Rama was only trying to attack those who were pointing out his flaws and mistakes.

The second week some more left because they felt that he was "monitoring" them and really had no business telling them what or how to examine other teachers or philosophies.

The third week some left because they did not like his style. Those of us who stayed (almost everyone) saw the point in his actions and eventually saw how perfectly he had presented this important lesson of non-judgment.

The Fast Path

Chapter Four – Higher Experiences

Meditation and the Wreck

Before I started studying with Rama, my life had disintegrated. I had lost my lucrative ministerial position, my marriage, and my children. I was alone. Now, after studying with Rama for only a couple of months, for the first time in my life, everything seemed perfect! Meditation, something that had always been difficult for me to do, suddenly became the easiest thing in the world. I was living in a state of Light that was constantly dissolving all the structures of my being. My realities were constantly shifting and I found it hard to live in the world.

I found myself unable to get any sort of work. I could no longer continue to be a minister. My heart was going in a new and completely different direction and it just did not seem right.

Finally, I landed a job selling automobile sheepskin seat covers.

"Mr. T's Sheepskins" was located at the corner of Santa Monica and Westwood (one of the busiest corners in Los Angeles). I swallowed my pride and decided that humility must be part of the experience of Enlightenment.

I found it ironic that a person with several advanced degrees should end up sitting on this street corner selling sheepskins. This was, however, the perfect job for me at that time. I experienced times of busy activity followed by long periods waiting for a customer. During the inactive times, I would sit in the shade on my lawn chair wearing my straw Panama hat and shades, and I would have wonderful meditations.

I experienced the entire street and buildings turn to gold as my attention started spanning the reaches of enlightened awareness. It was a gift from my teacher and I never grew tired of it. It seemed that his aura was with me constantly.

On this day, I was meditating with everything dissolved into gold, when there was a loud "Kabam!" As I heard the noise, I remembered taking a class years before, where the instructor said that noise was just energy, nothing more. I decided not to associate it with anything. Instead, I converted it into energy that would take me deeper into meditation. It worked!

People started to yell about calling the police. They scurried around, yelling and waving their arms. One individual even started directing traffic. I took this energy, too, and went deeper into my meditation.

Sirens came, fire trucks, then the police, then the ambulance. All this commotion and noise was just energy that I took deeper into my meditation.

The police directed traffic with their whistles and the ambulance took away the injured. More energy to take me deeper into God.

The fire trucks left and the wrecker came. The cars were hooked up and the street swept clean. Then the wrecker left.

Finally, the street slowly resumed its pattern of daily traffic. I was once again alone. I went deeper still.

The whole city was bathed in the most incredible white light.

It was a most extraordinary meditation.

This experience showed me that I did not need to meditate in absolute silence. Given the proper orientation, a person can have a wonderful meditation under the most distracting conditions.

I discovered that all sound and any other distraction is just energy. I give that energy shape with my thought. If these distractions are aimed toward God, then they propel me in that direction.

As I have related this experience to others, some have suggested that I should have left my meditation and tried to assist the victims. As a result, I have really examined whether or not I did the right thing.

I concluded that if I were ever in an auto accident and someone nearby was meditating, I would definitely want them to take that energy and go deeper into God. It seems to me that this is the proper use of energy and I am certain that everyone in the vicinity, including the victims, would benefit.

In The Desert

The desert was a little cool. It was in the late fall and I could see that it might be getting a little cold later on in the evening. I was glad that I had listened to Rama's advice as to what we should wear.

My fellow students and I had traveled to the Anza Borrego desert with Rama. I had been told that these outings were one of the most transformative experiences that we had with Rama.

I found a small pile of sand to sit down on and looked into the desert. I tried to meditate, but I was too excited and apprehensive. One never knew what would happen out there.

I had spent the last week tying up loose ends. I cleaned my apartment meticulously. I made sure that all my clothes were washed and neatly hung or folded in my dresser. I then wrote a letter to my friends and family telling them how much I appreciated all that they had done for me and how much I loved and wished them well. I made out a will and stated that I wanted to be cremated and to whom my personal belongings were to be distributed. This letter and will were placed in the dresser drawer along with my socks. In doing this, I felt that I had nothing holding me back or left unfinished.

I was determined to be ready to leave this world if it was time. Here I was sitting out in the desert ready to make whatever shifts needed to be made. I felt I had my life pretty tight.

Rama arrived and started walking up the desert. After about a half mile he stopped and gave us instructions as to the way we were to conduct ourselves during this trek. We then continued walking for another half mile. During this time, the mountains started to glow and undulate, almost as if they were taking huge deep breaths. Out of the corners of my eyes, I saw Indian-like figures standing on the cliffs overlooking the desert.

Rama stopped and had us look at a mountain. As we gazed at it, it disappeared! Then it reappeared. Rama had us look at him. He started to glow and seemed to change shape. He sat down in a lotus position. As I watched him, a rectangular blue object seemed to hover over him, turn, and shift, like some kind of computer graphic. I felt everything inside me tighten and goose bumps sprouted all over my arms.

When Rama stood up, he asked what we had just witnessed. I raised my hand and related what I had just seen. Rama's eyes lit up and he said, "Yes! You saw it! What did he just see?"

A woman standing a few feet away said, "It was your occult body."

I felt totally rattled, and yet, in spite of my agitated state, I knew that it was all so perfect.

Throughout the evening, I watched the stars swirl around and Rama disappear, grow large, and walk across the sand leaving no footprints. Later he shot energy out of his hand and lit up a mountain. I observed the moon bob around the sky like it was a kite on a string and then disappear into the cloudless sky for a few minutes.

At one point Rama started talking about the various winds. As he talked about the wind from the west and its qualities, a wind started blowing from the west. When he talked about the north wind, the wind shifted and started blowing from the north. Then the east and finally the south. Each time he would mention the various winds; there would be a gust of wind from that direction. It all seemed so natural and not at all unusual. It wasn't until later that I realized the full impact of what he had done!

Through all of the magic and displays of power, I had a sneaking sense that something else was happening inside. It was as if all these displays of spiritual power were just distractions to occupy our attention while some really powerful changes were taking place underneath.

After about four hours, we started walking out. The walk out seemed difficult to me. I had a hard time keeping myself oriented. The whole area seemed to me completely non-physical, only lines of energy and power configuring in unique ways and combinations of density.

When we reached the end of the path, Rama had us take a few minutes to review the night and to thank the desert.

The drive back home was a time for me to ground myself and reflect. I knew that some changes had been made but I was not aware what they might be.

I soon realized that any speculation I had about that evening did not even come close to the depth and impact it would have on my life!

After The Desert

It was a Sunday morning. I had slept in due to my late arrival home from being in the desert with Rama. I ambled into the kitchen to fix myself some breakfast. I was very sleepy.

I opened the door to the refrigerator and suddenly my stomach turned and I found myself wide-awake! I noticed that I had this uneasy, kind of queasy feeling every time I thought about eating anything that was meat or had meat in it.

It took me a couple of minutes of confusion before it all set in.

"Oh no, I'm a vegetarian!" I exclaimed. This was a calamity! I loved meat. I had always made fun of vegetarians. My refrigerator was stocked with ham, roast beef, steaks, hamburger, bacon, sausage, stews and other fine meat-laden food. I had never wanted to give up meat. I did not want to now!

I racked my brain and tried to think of what Rama had talked about in the desert. I was sure that he had not mentioned anything about being a vegetarian. I was confused and yet I knew this new development was a direct result of being in the desert with him.

As the day wore on, I resigned myself to this new role. I called over a couple of my friends and gave them most of the food in my refrigerator. They were happy as clams to get all of this great food.

It was so strange; being around meat did not bother me or make me feel funny. I did not mind being around other people eating meat. In fact, I envied them. I was only affected when I entertained the thought of eating meat myself. I was a forced vegetarian!

The strangeness did not end with the discovery of being a vegetarian. Rama was not done with me yet!

That afternoon I thought it would be nice to try out some of the restaurants that featured vegetarian food. I phoned one of my girlfriends, Anne. She sounded strange on the phone. As we talked, she said that she felt she could not continue in our relationship. She needed "space."

I then proceeded to call up my other girlfriends. Since my divorce, I had been enjoying a very active social life.

To my amazement, all my girlfriends were either moving out of town, moving back in with their old boyfriends or simply unavailable.

I finally sat my little black book down and meditated for a while. I wanted to see what was going on.

Then it hit me! I was not only a vegetarian, but I was also celibate!

For the next six months, I ate no meat, and to put it bluntly, could not score in a whorehouse. I learned to endure these forced changes and tried to observe my life. I perceived how being a vegetarian and celibate allowed me to retain more power and control over my thoughts and focus. Overall, I must say that it was a very effective change in my life.

After six months, I found myself in the desert with Rama again.

Between all the walking and the displays of power, during a rare quiet time, I realized inwardly that I now had a choice. The forced changes Rama had instituted were being lifted. I knew that I could remain a vegetarian or not. I also realized that I could remain celibate if I wanted to.

I considered the effects that being a vegetarian had on my life and I must say that I found them positive. I was not as creative as I used to be when it came to cooking, but I had managed to come up with some pretty good combinations of vegetarian cuisine. I felt great. I even lost a little unwanted weight. Therefore, I decided to remain vegetarian.

I then looked at being celibate. I felt that sexuality was one of the issues I came into this life to work out, and I decided to let go of my celibacy.

Rama never mentioned anything about being a vegetarian, nor did he breech the subject of sexuality during this desert trip.

However, I recognized that the doorway that had been closed months before was now open for me if I chose.

It was amazing! The next day after the desert trip, an old girlfriend returned from living up in northern California and gave me a call.

The Ebell Theater

I stood in the lobby of the Ebell Theater. I always liked this place. The old theater was built back in the early part of the century with large winding stairs and decorated elegantly.

Rama always tried to hold our meetings in beautiful places. The meeting halls had this special glow when we met.

As I stood on the stairway looking into the lobby taking in the beauty, a member of Rama's volunteer staff came up to me.

Rama had a select group of people who helped set up and organize the student meetings. I never was part of staff during my entire time with Rama. I always hoped that I would someday be able to help in setting up or assisting in some way.

"Hi! My name is David. I saw you over here and thought I would come over and introduce myself."

I was taken aback. Here I was actually talking to a student who associated with Rama in ways that I only dreamed of and I really did not know what to say.

"Hi!" I answered trying to appear cool. "My, this is a beautiful building."

We stood there in silence looking it over. It seemed like a nice moment, but I was eager to impress him.

"I used to be a minister in Beverly Hills and I held my services in this theater every Sunday," I said.

He looked at me, let out a quick breath, shook his head and walked away.

I got it! No wonder I was not allowed to be part of the staff. My ego was so immense that it just could not wait to run wild. I sure felt like a complete ass.

David was a great teacher to me that evening.

The Fast Path

Chapter Five – Personal Encounters

So, You Want To Be A Teacher?

The student meeting this particular evening was being held in the Beverly Theater in Beverly Hills. Throughout the evening, I felt an agitation in my heart increasing. I had felt this stirring for over a week. During the meditation I suddenly became aware of what it was that was burning inside me.

During the break, I waited in the theater lobby. Rama sometimes walked around and made himself available to us this way. After a while, I spotted him and I quietly approached him and waited for an appropriate time to gain his attention. I waited patiently until he finished talking to another student. As he turned away, I said his name out loud. His name is a mantra and I said it as such.

He turned and faced me. I felt myself starting to dissolve. I was determined to state my intention.

"Rama, I would like to be a teacher." I blurted out.

He said, "Of course you do."

I stood my ground. I asked, "When?"

This question gained his attention. I felt him look even deeper into me.

"There is much more to teaching than you realize. In order to teach, a person needs to be able to look deeply into those he meets. The teacher should be able to 'see' the aura of his students and to assess the damage and tears that the individual has on their subtle physical body. He needs to have the ability to evaluate the emotional body; is it out of control or unstable? How about the occult body? Where in the body does it manifest most of its power? How powerful is it? A teacher needs to be able to look at the past-life development in order to see karmic influences and gain insight into the general direction the soul seems to be taking. What about the causal body? It's important to have the ability to evaluate the potential that the individual is capable of realizing in this life.

"It is only when a teacher can account for all of these different variables that a really effective series of techniques and recommendations can be made. If a teacher starts to teach before this awareness develops, then he will just be dealing with the surface and that is not usually very effective and can even be counterproductive and destructive."

I stood there finally grasping all that was involved in my request. I was overwhelmed and painfully aware at how little I could see or was even aware of.

Rama sensed this and smiled and said, "Just hang around. I am sure that as time goes by you will begin to see all these things. In the meantime just keep up your meditation."

I felt a deep-seated appreciation for his abilities and insight. I also had an increased awareness into how Rama was able to deal with people such as myself.

As I walked away, I still wanted to teach. The desire was even greater now that I saw how exciting it would be once I could do all the things Rama said. I had a long way to go. I knew that I would need to wait until the right time and until I had developed these skills to be effective.

I had no idea that my association with Rama would create such advanced states of awareness in an incredibly short period!

The Visit

It was a long hard day. As I punched out my time card, I was exhausted.

I was working at the Fleetwood Motor Home Manufacturing Plant in Riverside. This day seemed harder than most. It had been blistering hot. In addition, we had worked on the larger coaches. It seemed that we worked twice as hard on days like this.

It must have been close to a hundred degrees as I drove home. I was so tired that my mind seemed numb.

There was a student meeting tonight. Only enough time to shower, get dressed and hit the traffic into Beverly Hills where the student meetings were being held. I was so weary that the thought occurred that I needed to rest. It might be dangerous to drive after such a hard day. Rama would understand that...

"Bullshit!" I shouted in the car. I was determined not to let my ego keep me from a meditation with my teacher! Suddenly the weight lifted and I felt energized.

As I pulled up in front of my brother's home (I was living with him at the time), I saw my parents' car. They had come out for a surprise visit from New Mexico!

I walked into the house and was greeted by these wonderful people that I truly loved. Mom had fried up some chicken and set the table with gravy, mashed potatoes, green beans and hot rolls! My favorite meal! This was awful! The temptation was great to push through my meat-eating aversion.

I hugged my parents, got a change of clothes and showered. I informed them that I had an important meeting that I had to attend and that they should rest. I assured them that we would visit in the morning. I could see the look of disappointment cross over my parents faces as I grabbed a hot roll and left.

It was the most amazing student meeting I had attended in months! I attained states of awareness that I could never have imagined! I was so glad that I had pushed through circumstances and my own resistance to make the meeting.

The next morning I did the family thing. Mom and Dad seemed okay with my not staying home the night before. I was glad that they took it that way. As I said, they are extraordinary and I really love them.

This also provided me with an experience in seeing my priorities at the time. It was one of the high points in my self-discovery process.

The Golden Oldies

It was a foggy night on the Pomona Freeway as I headed toward Riverside. Traffic was sparse due to the lateness of the hour. It was almost 2 a.m. and I was still meditating.

Rama had ended the student meeting around 1:30 and I had to get up at 6 a.m. to work on the motor home assembly line. I wasn't tired or worried about tomorrow; I was energized and sleep wasn't a concern.

I drove in silence for a while and then decided to see if there was anything on the radio. The radio in my car soon picked up a station playing "Golden Oldies."

As I listened to the songs that were popular during my high school and college years, I was fascinated by the fact that I no longer felt any emotions or strong associations with the past. I sang "Unchained Melody" along with the Righteous Brothers and did not feel the person I used to date or any of the memories that always came forth when I used to sing or listen to that song. "Surfer Girl" by the Beach Boys, one of the songs from my high school days, was just another fun song to sing along with. I sat amazed as I realized that I had no emotionally charged memories or associations with these songs from my distant past. Song after song, I knew the tunes and words, but no emotional attachment!

I grinned and sang out loud as I barreled down that dark freeway. I had been set free! Free from the past and the emotional ties that held me back. I felt liberated! I did not understand it, but I was happier than I had ever been. I could not believe how fortunate I was to experience life in this extraordinary way.

The Correction

After studying with Rama for almost a year, I witnessed my spiritual community go through a rough time.

It seems that a large group of students were displaying some sloppy habits and lacking spiritual etiquette. Rama dealt severely not only with the etiquette problems but also with this negative attitude and state of mind that just seemed to hang around. The atmosphere at the meditations was, at times, very thick, full of anger and distress. It was as if there were a power struggle going on between Rama and some of his students.

On this particular evening, everyone entered the meditation hall with some trepidation. During the last few meetings, we had been treated to serious dissertations on spiritual etiquette. These comments were met with a mixture of anger and upset by the students. It was strange to witness this taking place in the dissolving golden light of Samadhi.

Strangely, I found these evenings to be some of the best meditations so far. Since I did not identify with the students who were being negative, I took the energy in the room and transformed it by taking it in and moving it up through my being. I found that it changed its quality as it moved up through the various chakras.

Toward the end of this period, Rama entered and finally seemed to be in a good space. Rama said that he felt that maybe we had gotten the message. He then reviewed all that had been presented during the previous weeks. Everyone was very uptight and yet I could sense that they were finally happy and ready to put this period behind us. Rama smiled and asked if there were any questions.

The room was very tense. Nobody wanted to risk opening their mouths. I felt somewhat relieved that the storm was now over. I wanted to lighten up things. I raised my hand.

"Yes?" he said as he looked at me.

"As a result of the past few weeks, are we still going to be able to get our rings?" I ventured, referring to a possible gift he had offered some weeks before.

There was a nervous laughter in the room.

"That is precisely the attitude I have been talking about!" he said as he pointed his finger at me. "I can't believe that after all that has come down, you call still ask such a question!"

Rama continued for over fifteen minutes. I was exposed, laid out for all to see. My elitist, self-righteous attitude was openly exposed and I was defenseless. My heart was broken. How could I have missed it? I refused to ego-justify myself. I had been caught and now it was time to face the full force of Eternity. I truly felt naked.

As he continued talking, I opened my heart as wide as I could to my teacher. I knew this was the correction needed. I began to meditate as he continued to blast me. Suddenly I was transported into a state of mind that was extraordinary. I was aware of the thoughts and emotions of everyone in the room, not just the sum total of their thoughts, but each person's thoughts. I was shocked to find that many of the students felt that I was being unfairly singled out. Some were even angrier with Rama for what they perceived to be brutish tactics. I wanted to tell them to stop! They could not perceive what was going on with me during this time. I rose to even greater heights of awareness that transcended the room and felt that I was approaching the awareness of Rama. I was truly humbled and ashamed. How could I take such a cavalier attitude toward Enlightenment? Soon I found myself returning to the awareness of the room where Rama was still talking to me. As I opened my eyes, he finally stopped and said with a wiry smile, "There may be some hope for you yet."

I was grateful for this last statement. I felt love for my teacher and for the correction. As the students rose to leave for a break, I could still feel them and their thoughts. Some looked at me with disgust, others with sadness or pity. I could not move. I was still in deep meditation. I was acutely aware of all that had transpired and determined that I would immediately put into practice the various changes that clearly had to take place. I was also aware that Rama had somehow given me an empowerment that would make it possible to make the needed changes quickly.

Overall, I felt that this was one of the high points of my time with Rama.

The Gift

I stood in the lobby of the Beverly Theater during a break. I was happy and a little sad at the same time. I was happy that Rama had announced that we would be going on an outing to Disneyland. I was sad that I would not be able to include my two boys.

I was having a hard time financially and I just barely had enough money to go myself. I certainly did not have the means to take my children.

I stood next to the wall and thought about how Rama had said that we were all getting a little up tight.

"Life is too short not to enjoy the trip," he exclaimed! "We need to lighten up! I feel that it is time to do something that is happy and childlike. We're going to Disneyland!"

The students laughed and applauded.

"Disneyland is a world within worlds. Each one is so perfect!" he continued. "The people at Disneyland always make sure that the park is impeccable. The various worlds of Adventureland, Tomorrowland, Frontierland and the rest are like small worlds in a greater Universe. We will have so much fun!"

Now here I was alone in a crowded lobby trying to figure out a way to go on this outing and have my boys with me. I looked up just in time to see Rama stroll toward me.

"How's it going?" he asked with a big smile.

I felt myself dissolving and it was hard to keep my thoughts straight as I struggled with my answer.

"It's going OK," I blurted out.

"Just OK?" he queried.

I was trapped. I knew that my best course of action was to open my heart and tell the truth. "I am really looking forward to going to Disneyland," I said. "I was just trying to figure out a way to take my sons with me. I am going to pull some strings and see if I can make it happen. If not, perhaps next time," I said.

Rama looked at me and reached into his pockets. Realizing that they were empty, he turned and motioned for one of his staff to come over. He whispered something to the man who then immediately fished out his wallet and handed Rama some money. Rama turned to me and handed me a wad of bills.

"Take this and I'll see you at Disneyland with your boys," he said with a smile.

As he turned a walked away, I stared in disbelief as I looked in my hand. There was more than enough money for all of us to go. Not only would my boys be able to go with me, but also we could buy some souvenirs! This would really be fun now! I started to get a lump in my throat and my eyes started to fill with tears of joy as I considered the way Rama had tuned in and found me. I was speechless.

Disneyland

Anyone who has ever gone to Disneyland with two wide-eyed, six and eight year old boys can fully understand how magical Disneyland can really be! I was delighted in looking at this wonderland through their eyes. Chad insisted on carrying his "Snoopy" and his younger brother, Lonnie, had to have "Clyde" (a funny stuffed vulture). I do not think I have ever enjoyed the day as much as I did that one. Each section to the theme park we went into, I would watch my boys transform into the dream. Amazingly, I had just as much energy as they did.

Only one thing, all during the day, I never once saw Rama. I could feel him, but our paths did not cross. Finally, it was time to go. As I started walking out of the park, I felt certain that we would meet Rama at the exit gate. Somehow, I felt that we had met each other at the exit gate many times at the end of my lives.

Sure enough, there he stood with a few friends. My sons and I went over to Rama and he bent down and looked at each boy. He asked each one about their time at Disneyland. Their eyes sparkled as they described their adventures. Finally, he asked them about their stuffed animals. Reluctantly they each gave him their most prized possession. He held each animal and them smiled as he handed them back. Both boys grinned and we said good-bye.

What a day!

Up to this day, both of my sons, now fully grown and living on their own, still have those stuffed toys. It is a reminder of a day in a magical kingdom with an Enlightened teacher.

The Fast Path

Chapter Six – A New Beginning

The Letter

On Tuesday, the letter arrived. I held it with my trembling hands. Curiosity and apprehension gripped me. This was the most important letter I had ever received. I excused myself from the family, went to my room, and sat down in front of my meditation table. I took a deep breath before I opened the envelope.

During the past three months, my spiritual community had been involved in a great transition. The result was turmoil that resulted in anxiety, resentment and even anger. Groups and individuals had misused their power and the resulting political atmosphere became thick and unhappy.

Rama was not happy with the way this transition was being handled, and informed the students that he realized that he had too many students. He felt that he needed to look closely into each one of us and then he would decide who would benefit the most from actively studying with him. In this way those who needed some time to grow on their own, away from the energy of the spiritual community, would be forced out of the nest. Everyone would receive a letter either saying whether they could stay or not.

This was very serious. Anyone who was asked to leave could not return to the spiritual community or have any contact with the students for at least one year and maybe never!

I did not feel that I was in any great trouble in that I had always attended the events and tried not to be involved with the students who were focusing on Rama's personal life and the social atmosphere of the various student groups. I attended for one reason. I wanted Enlightenment. In fact, I rarely was able to attend any of the social functions such as group movies because of my circumstance of living so far away. I would drive seventy

miles through Los Angeles traffic just to attend a meditation.
I really was focused on spiritual quest and just didn't care about who was dating whom and how much money so-and-so was making. I went because at every meditation I dissolved with my teacher into golden light. My whole life had really become centered on meditating with Rama.

I held in my hands the letter on which my whole life now hinged. I took a deep breath and opened the letter.

My world stopped!

"Dear Tony,

You are no longer a part of the spiritual community..."

How could this be? The letter went on but my tears blurred it out.

My mind wandered and for a moment, my ego flared. My emotions welled up as they did when I was a child, and had been wronged. How could this be? All I wanted was the Light! I was not interested in all the negativity that so many of the students seemed to thrive on. I was not upset or angry with anyone! I had really tried to keep it clean with my practice and with my inner association with Rama. How could this be? Rama is wrong! I did nothing! There must be some mistake!

I caught myself and stopped the indulging.

"Has the last year meant anything to me?" I asked myself. "Did I trust the insight and wisdom of Rama before the letter?" The answer was "Absolutely!"

Then, I reasoned, if Rama saw something deep inside that needed to be worked out, I guess I had better start figuring out ways to uncover it and correct it!

This did not do much in easing my acute disappointment but at least I had my emotional body under control as I went out to the kitchen to give my brother the news.

Warren was not only my brother but also a strong supporter of my spiritual endeavors. He had done anything he could to help me during my year with Rama. He seemed to have an understanding of the process and always seemed to do or say the right thing when it came time. As I broke the news to him, I could see the disappointment on his face.

The next morning Warren asked me, over breakfast, what I was going to do now that I was no longer a student. I said I really had not given it very much thought. Rama had outlined a recommended course of action we should take in the event of our dismissal. It involved taking a brief inventory of our life and trying to ascertain the direction that this incarnation was taking us. I decided to do this on my next day off.

"Good!" he said. "By the way, I am starting a meditation class at the church tonight and since you have studied Transcendental Meditation, Zen meditation and other forms of meditation, not to mention having just finished a year with an Enlightened teacher, I thought that maybe you could teach it."

"Oh no!" I exclaimed. "I wouldn't presume to do that!"

"Fine, I understand. I will do it myself. Let me know if you change your mind," he said smiling as he walked out the door.

All day while working at the motor home factory, I thought about what he had said. I thought about the people who would be showing up to the meditation class. I knew I could never teach at the level of Rama. However, I was more qualified to teach than my brother did.

That afternoon I asked Warren if the offer was still good.

"But of course!" he exclaimed happily.

I spent the next couple of hours gathering up materials that I felt I would need in presenting the class. I showed up with charts and recommended books to read. I organized the music and had my lesson plan all laid out. I took a breath as the people started to fill the room.

The class went well until I asked everyone to sit up straight and we would meditate for a few moments.

I started the music and suddenly the world went away. I was caught up in a powerful meditation that, up until that time, I had only experienced with Rama! I simply went into God! I went deeper and deeper until there was no more me. I can't describe what happened then because it is impossible to connect or reference with anything in this reality.

At the end of the meditation, I opened my eyes to a room full of people who were staring at me with their eyes bugged out and their mouths opened. Obviously, Rama had given me some sort of empowerment during my time with him! I was astonished!

Everyone was enthusiastic and wanted to attend more classes. I said I would talk it over with my brother. After all, it was his church.

The following Saturday I traveled to Keyes View in the Joshua Tree National Park. Keyes View was my second choice because Rama was going to be with his students at my favorite place of power in the Anza Borrego Desert.

I found a secluded spot out of view from the public and sat on a nice rock. For a moment, I indulged in a sense of longing to be with Rama, but I realized that this sort of self-indulgence was counterproductive.

I closed my eyes and once again became an impeccable student. I reviewed in my mind what Rama had said to do if we were ever asked to leave. I wished I had paid more attention. It just never occurred to me that I had anything to worry about. I supposed I felt that I would always be a student. Once again, I had to stop indulging.

Then I started to follow his recommendations in reviewing my life. I proceeded to take stock of my inventory of resources, then attempted to determine the direction I needed go.

I reviewed my whole life from childhood to the present. I saw what life had presented to me in the way of my family and their profound influence on me. I examined the various jobs I had in the past, and why I was drawn me to them. I reviewed my education, both formal and informal, and all of my love relationships from early childhood to the present. I recalled my spiritual pathway, the epiphanies and the growth I experienced.

As the sun began to set and the stars began to fill the sky, my whole life seemed to meld into a glorious quest. I saw at a deep level how there had been no wasted motion. A lifetime of religious involvement, sales experience, teaching, counseling and coaching, could be best used as a minister. It was perfect that I had been a minister in a New Age church that encouraged meditation.

I could even teach meditation as a class in my church!

I was both apprehensive and excited about the direction I was now headed. I did not fully understand why I had been asked to leave, but at least I did not allow my ego to justify itself and trash Rama or my fellow students.

I thought of Rama in the desert to the south of me and in my heart of hearts, I thanked him for the last year. I then rose, said good-bye to Keyes View and headed for my car and a whole new adventure.

Starting Out

I pulled my loaded pickup into the parking lot at Point Dune, my favorite beach in Malibu. I often came here to meditate. I knew that Rama lived in Malibu, but I did not know where.

I did like this beach. There is a large rock at the end of the beach and I liked to climb onto some of the small outcroppings that jutted out toward the sea. Here I would meditate and contemplate and just plain sort things out.

A couple of months before, I had been unexpectedly asked to leave my study with Rama. Now I had accepted a position as a minister in Grants Pass, Oregon. That is why my old Ford pickup was loaded and why I was here.

I was leaving California, my teacher and a way of life and awareness that few people could ever fathom. It was time to move ahead into whatever life had in store for me.

I came here to Malibu to say good-bye. It was a little cold and the sunset was beautiful. I sat and thought about Rama, my experiences with him and how this past year had impacted me. It was astonishing to look at what had happened!

I said good-bye to all that had happened and my old way of life. Then I thought about Rama. I inwardly apologized for any hurt or trouble I may have caused him. I trusted his judgment and knew that one day I would see why I was having to take this path. I wished him well and thanked him.

I set out on the adventure of my new life.

First Night as a Teacher

I walked into the meditation hall. I had started out as the minister in Grants Pass, Oregon only two weeks before. Interest in meditation seemed to be high. It was only last Sunday that I had announced that I would be starting a class in meditation on Tuesday night.

Now here they were over fifty people! The room was absolutely packed. I had no idea so many would show up!

As I sat down, I was a little overwhelmed. I looked at the souls in front of me through extended awareness. I knew that I had my work cut out for me. I would have to draw deeply from my experiences with Rama. I was grateful that he had empowered me to handle this task.

I turned on the music and the world dissolved into golden light.

Over the next two years, I began to see why Rama had asked me to leave in the way he did. I realized that if Rama had pulled me aside and said, "Tony, there is a large group of students I know of in Grants Pass that need a teacher and I am going to send you," my ego would have been out of control. I would have constantly bothered him with every little problem and developed a horrible, elitist attitude. As it was, I had to figure it all out for myself, and either fly or fall. I could not talk to him or any of his students. It is hard to develop an elitist attitude when you have been exiled. The result of being on my own was a tremendous push forward.

The following three years I taught meditation seminars throughout California, Oregon and Idaho. This experience caused me to draw from deep within while performing this wonderful activity. I cannot say that I did not make mistakes and stumble occasionally, but overall it was the most powerful assignment I could have undertaken.

Now I began to understand why I was put in exile.

The Thank You Card

It was a beautiful day in Grants Pass. I walked up the gravel road to the mailbox. My mind began to wander back on the last few weeks. I had been teaching in Grants Pass for over six months now and I was happier than I could ever remember.

I had recently dealt with some students who wanted to make Rama wrong for not letting me continue my study with him. As usual, I would not have anyone, especially my students, trash Rama. I had told them that their judgments were off base and that they had no idea how an enlightened mind worked. While I did not fully understand everything that Rama did, I trusted his judgment implicitly.

I still felt a sense of having let Rama down or not measuring up to his expectations. I missed the student meetings and meditating with him. Now I was over fourteen hundred miles away and I felt that I was far from being a good teacher. It was hard because I was constantly flying by the seat of my pants. I always wondered if I was doing the right thing or if I was getting off course.

I opened the mailbox and there, among the bills and junk mail, was this small envelope. I ripped open the envelope and removed the card, which said, "Thank You!" A rush of energy and light washed over me as I opened the card to see it simply signed, "Rama."

I laughed and cried at the same time. What a gift. I did not understand how Rama knew that I needed that confirmation at that time. It was one of the most wonderful gifts I had ever received!

Chapter Seven – Back on the Saddle

Priorities

My period of exile had just ended and I received an invitation to Los Angeles to attend a public meditation with Rama. I journeyed from Oregon for this three-day seminar and eagerly looked forward to seeing and meditating with Rama again!

It was hard to believe that I was here once again in a large room with over fourteen hundred people registering and about to finally sit with my teacher again!

At the registration table, one of the women said, "Didn't you used to be a student?"

"Yes," I said. "I've been in Oregon, and Rama said I could once again attend the open meditations." She left and conferred with some other students and returned, smiled and welcomed me.

I noticed that I seemed to be the object of discussion with some of the women students. One even looked and pointed at me as they were talking.

I had known these women from my time before as a student. I really had little to do with them then and couldn't quite understand why they were paying me so much attention now. Finally, a heavy-set woman approached me and said, "Aren't you the one who has been teaching in Oregon?" I nodded yes and she left. I found my chair about three quarters of the way back.

It felt so good to feel Rama's energy like this once again. I started to meditate and once again enjoyed feeling the waves of energy sweep through the crowd.

Then this same woman moved through the crowd and sat next to me. I was a little uncomfortable, but I soon drifted back into meditation.

Rama entered and I focused totally upon him. I tried to be just with him, and no one else. This was not easy as I was keenly aware of this woman sitting next to me. Still, I pushed her out of my attention and focused on Rama. Rama told us to sit up straight and we would meditate.

Then the woman did the most extraordinary thing! She moved her chair so that she was at a forty-five degree angle to Rama and me! I had to move my knees in order not to touch her. I could not believe it! This was one of the most rude actions that I had ever encountered as a student.

I closed my eyes and wondered if I should move. She would follow me, I decided. What could I do?

Rama said, "Focus on your purpose in being here tonight."

"Of course!" I thought. I did not travel fourteen hundred miles to focus on an incredibly rude student. I came to meditate on Rama. I focused on him and mentally pushed her away. Still, I could not fathom why anyone would attend a meditation with Rama and spend even a second focusing on me! Her priorities seemed to be a little skewed in this case.

With great difficulty, I succeeded in pushing through this distraction during the meditation and waited for the break.

At the end of the break, I spotted a seat with people on both sides. I grabbed it and was able to spend the rest of the meditation without interference.

Looking back, I am still amazed that this individual displayed such rudeness and a breech of spiritual etiquette. Most of all, I cannot fathom why she would waste her time focusing on me when Rama was in the room! Having been away from my teacher made me realize just how precious each moment was with him. It was all beyond me. I could only assume that her priorities were very different from mine.

I also realized that the reason there are students is because individuals need to learn a body of knowledge. Just because someone is a student of an Enlightened teacher doesn't mean that they are perfect. I knew that I certainly wasn't. In fact, the argument could be made that students of an Enlightened teacher are usually far from perfect. Their saving grace is that they have been drawn into a field of awareness that allows for a doorway into Enlightenment.

Corrected Again

Interstate 5 is a long straight stretch of divided highway that goes for hundreds of miles through central California. It was just the type of road I liked. It gave me lots of time to sort things out and time to practice seeing how long I could stop my thoughts. On this trip, I was certainly sorting things out.

A couple of weeks back I had received notice of an up-coming mediation seminar in Los Angeles. I had attended several meditations during the past few months. In fact, I had not missed one of Rama's public seminars after my year of exile. This particular seminar could not have come at a better time.

I thought about my situation back in Grants Pass. For the past few months, I seemed to have gotten off track. It was a subtle change that had slowly become a huge problem.

Over the months, I had attracted various people to my meditation class. Some of them practiced Kundalini Yoga, others practiced Siddha Yoga, and others followed the practices of Zen.

Some of these students thought it would be a good idea to hold a preparatory yoga session right before my meditation.

At first this worked out fine, but now people were showing up an hour and a half early to participate in Kundalini Yoga and then have a satsang [2] with the Siddha group. Many times, I had to wait for the room to be cleared and set up before I was even able to enter. In short, it was becoming a real mess. Everything seemed out of control and I did not really know what to do.

As I drove, I knew how Rama held his seminars; I could not imagine him ever participating in the circus I was involved in.

The following evening, I parked my car and came up the steps to the Design Center in Beverly Hills. This was a beautiful building and the meeting rooms were wonderful!

Rama met me just outside the door.

"How are you doing?" he asked. I felt myself dissolving.

"I'm fine," I said shakily. He turned and started walking inside with me. I was withering under his energy.

"Well, actually that's not quite right. I'm trying to sort out some situations I have been experiencing."

"Well, you've come to the right place to sort things out. Good luck!" he said as he walked away.

The following two nights were powerful and magical, but I still did not have a clear answer. On the third and final night, Rama once again met me at the door.

"Well have you received an answer to your dilemma?"

He turned and walked with me inside the door. Here, waiting for him, were some of his better students. I admired these people. They were far cleaner than I was, and were fortunate enough to be a part of the staff. My ego blossomed as we approached them. Now they would see that I had this "special connection" with Rama.

---

[2] A satsang typically involves listening to or reading scriptures, reflecting on, discussing and assimilating their meaning, meditating on the source of these words, and bringing their meaning into one's daily life.

"No," I replied, "but maybe tonight."

Rama took about four steps, placing him right in front of his students. Then he turned to face me. He had that look in his eyes. I felt it coming.

"You had better watch out! You're on thin ice around here!" he said. Your ego is so large that you seek approval from everyone around you! You had better snap out of it! This over-inflated ego of yours makes you a slave to whomever happens to be around. You are afraid to do anything that might alienate someone or cause them to disapprove of you. This constant need for the gratitude and approval of others forces you to bend and even submit to their wishes! You had better straighten out this messy situation right away or else you will lose it all! Get with it!" He then turned and walked away.

As he was talking to me, he was also snapping his fingers. With each snap, I felt jolts of energy shoot through me. I opened my heart. This was what I had come down for. The answer did not come in the way I would have thought, but there it was. I had been exposed in front of those that I wanted to impress. I had been exposed in front of the universe! He had me stone cold.

I sat down, and meditated on every word and realized how correct he had been. I knew that I had to make changes and regain control of my meditation dojo. I was also aware that this correction was accompanied by an empowerment that would help me.

I resolved to do what my teacher said, not because he said it, but because I saw and realized deep within my heart that he was absolutely correct. This correction went far beyond my expectations. Rama had dealt with me impeccably and words could not say how much this meant to me. Only my actions during the following days would show it.

Returning Home

Interstate 5 stretched out ahead of me like a double gray ribbon with gentle rolling hills on my left and the San Joaquin Valley on my right. I was returning home after a three-day meditation seminar with Rama.

For the last three days, Rama had spent a great deal of time talking about how important it was to view everything unemotionally.

"There is clarity to perception when we can remove the distortions of emotions," he said.

As I drove along, I wondered how that could be. All my life I viewed everything through feelings. My memories were not made of visual images. They consisted of how things felt. I remembered being four years old and in my mother's kitchen. I could feel songs and storybooks that were part of my life at the time and how they colored my perception. I vividly remembered how the room seemed to be alive with feeling. I had a variety of comforting feelings as I watched my mother prepare a meal. I recalled the pleasing smell of her cooking, and how I felt. I was in touch with the whole atmosphere of my life at that moment. Every piece of furniture, the house, our car at the time, everything, was a feeling. These recollections had far more depth than just a visual image. All this was done through an intense, sensuous recollection of feelings that invoked emotions.

So how could I ever expect to experience life unemotionally? I decided that I would never be able to, and just let it be.

I practiced stopping my thoughts for a few miles. Then I fell into a mode of just driving.

North of Sacramento I looked out to the rolling hills and the beautiful mountains in the distance. The sky was this incredible blue and everything seemed crystal clear. In fact, I was amazed at how clear everything was, including my thoughts. I thought about my students and the meditation classes and outings I had planned. It all seemed so clear as to which direction I should go and exactly how to handle some pretty ticklish situations.

Then it hit me! I had spent this last ten minutes without any emotions! So this is what it is like, I thought unemotionally. I was more at ease, more at peace and definitely more in control of my mind. I was amazed at how easy it was to stop my thoughts and keep them quiet.

Rama had been right about this emotion thing. Now that I had first-hand knowledge, it was incredible. I did not understand how he did it, but the ability to remember, see and experience life from this unemotional level was something I could never have conceived of doing. Now here I was doing it! Pretty incredible!

Chapter Eight – Moving to the East

The Call

It was a beautiful Saturday morning and I was excited about next week's meditation in La Jolla. I was traveling down from Riverside with one of my students, Tracy. The week before, I had arranged by telephone to rent the Women's Club meeting hall, and now it was time to complete the agreement and put up the posters.

Tracy had just been accepted as a student of Rama and I was excited for her. We talked about her up-coming move to New York.

"Tony, why don't you apply? I bet Rama would accept you back in a minute!" she said excitedly.

"Not me," I said. "I have crossed over into being a teacher. I cannot go back and be a student again. Besides, I'm sure that things will start working out for me here real soon."

We traveled in silence for a while. My mind started to drift. I had been teaching for three years now. What I did not tell Tracy was that I was very concerned about my level of consciousness.

Over a year ago, I had resigned from my church in Grants Pass. I finally realized that church politics is one area of my life that I no longer wanted to deal with. For the past year, I traveled on a circuit holding monthly meditations in Idaho, Oregon, and California where I visited Palo Alto, Santa Barbara, Los Angeles, and Riverside. Now I was trying to add La Jolla. It was a busy but fulfilling life.

However, lately it seemed that my meditations had leveled out. It had become a nagging concern that I could not share with anybody. The only thing I knew to do was to continue holding meditation seminars.

"New York is not the place for me," I said. "I love being out west. I can't imagine moving back east."

"What if Rama called you up and said, 'Come to New York.' What would you do?" Tracy queried.

I honestly did not know. I was scared to death that he might and then I would be forced to leave my students and everything else. It was comforting to know that Rama never made such calls, at least not to my knowledge.

We arrived in La Jolla and started putting up the posters. As Tracy and I walked across the park, there was small band playing a song. "That's so strange to hear a band in La Jolla playing the song 'New York, New York,'" Tracy said. Something in my navel twinged. Everything was going fine until she said that.

I told Tracy that I needed to mail a letter. I walked over to the Post Office and through the door. As I waited for a window, I started humming a tune and then I began to sing it. It was a catchy little tune, I had not sung in over twenty years.

"East Side, West Side, all around the tow... OH SHIT!" I said out loud. Everyone in the Post Office turned and looked at me. One middle-aged woman glared at me with extreme disapproval because of my language. I did not care! Rama had done it again! I had been called to New York! I knew! Nothing else needed to be said. My life as I knew it was over. Everything was ashes.

On the drive home, I related this to Tracy. I thought she never would stop laughing. She laughed at the way Rama had called me. She laughed at my reaction in the Post Office, but most of all, she was laughing at my state of mind as I drove home to Riverside. I was a real mess.

On The Road to New York

Mom and Dad were great! I had left Riverside just two days before and had stopped by Carlsbad, New Mexico to leave my car with my oldest son, Chad. I was told by people who had never been to, much less lived in, New York that I would not need a car there.

I had arranged through a drive-away agency to deliver an automobile to New London, Connecticut. The only problem was that the car was in Albuquerque, about two hundred miles away.

Mom and Dad packed up all of my belongings that could fit into their car and drove me. They did not like the idea of my traveling so far away, but they were doing everything in their power to help me.

We picked up the car and dad pulled me aside.

"How much money do you have?" he asked.

"I have two hundred and fifty dollars," I replied.

Dad reached inside his pocket and handed me fifty dollars.

"Your mother doesn't know that I had this socked away. I want you to take it and don't let her know that I gave it to you."

I fought back the tears. My dad was over seventy years old. This was an enormous amount of money to him.

A few minutes later Mom pulled me aside.

"Here, take this and don't let your dad know that I gave it to you. He doesn't know I had it put away." It was another fifty dollars. This was so touching I could hardly choke out a thank you.

They then took me out to eat at a Mexican restaurant. I savored every moment with them. I was not sure that I would ever see them again. They were so old and frail. I had no idea how or when I would ever make it back to see them.

Mom and Dad helped me load the car and had me follow them to a Shell station. There they filled up my car. Once again, they talked quietly, then dad came over and handed me Mom's gasoline credit card.

"We don't want you using up all your money on gas. Take this card and you can pay us back when you are rich and famous," he grinned.

I was almost forty-three years old when I left Albuquerque for New York to study with my teacher once again. I had three hundred and fifty dollars and my Mom's gasoline card, but I felt rich. My parents' extraordinary show of unconditional love had left me profoundly moved.

I was starting out on the greatest adventure of my life. I was scared and excited. I had never been east of Oklahoma City. It was a whole new world...

On my way to New York, I remembered Rama saying that in India, when a son went off to study with an Enlightened teacher, the family held a big party. They knew that if they supported the direction that their son was going, it would mean incredible good luck for the family.

During the three years I lived in New York, my parents had three financial windfalls of over forty thousand dollars each. When I returned from New York, they owned their house along with three rental houses and a trailer park. Their new car was paid for along with a new pick-up. They had over fifty thousand dollars in the bank. They were living better than they had lived in their life! Rama was right once again.

Christmas at Golden's Bridge

It was Christmas Eve. I had to work that day as a telephone solicitor. It was stupid. Nobody buys recycled laser printer cartridges on Christmas Eve! However, my boss, being the modern-day Scrooge that he was, refused to give me the day off. After a frustrating day of getting answering machines and switchboards, I was finally headed home.

I had only recently moved to New York to continue my study with Rama. This was my first Christmas away from family and friends. I was forty-three and it was quite an adventure for a man who had never been east of Dallas.

I was staying with a group of fellow students. We shared a large house in Golden's Bridge (about an hour's train ride north of New York City). It was true country living. The house was located about seven miles back into the woods. The place was very quiet and secluded.

This particular time, being Christmas Eve, I was looking forward to getting home and having some hot tea with my friends around the fire. Why, there might even be a party! I also wanted to phone my family. My parents had traveled from New Mexico to California in order to be with my sons and brothers for the holidays. A phone call to them would be nice.

I got off the train at Golden's Bridge (a good distance from the house). The ground was covered with about three inches of powdery snow. It was incredibly silent and beautiful, just like a Christmas card.

I located a phone and called the house. No one answered, just a cold, impersonal voice on the machine asking that I leave a message.

I waited and continued to call every fifteen minutes. I had no car, and not enough money for a cab home. It was eight miles from the station to the house. Around seven o'clock the snow had stopped falling and the temperature began to drop. I continued to phone. It was now eight o'clock and I had been at the station for over two hours.

Strangely, I did not feel depressed or upset. I sang a few Christmas carols and made some snowballs, and kept on calling.

Finally, I walked to a nearby supermarket and called from there. At nine o'clock, they closed and I had to wait outside.

I could not imagine what had happened to all my roommates. However, I refused to allow myself to be depressed.

I played in the snow, made a small snowman and sang some more.

There was a time when I thought about all the people around me who were enjoying Christmas. I thought about my family, and how I loved them.

Still, strange as it seems, I was not depressed or frustrated. I simply refused to allow myself to indulge in those emotional states. I kept busy building snowmen and playing soccer in the snow with an old box for a ball.

At eleven thirty on Christmas Eve, my roommate showed up. He was most apologetic. Everyone had gone to different parties and they each thought I had been at another party.

I smiled as I climbed into his warm car. I was tired, but I was not upset. I said, "These things happen."

At midnight, I sat in my warm room with my tea, and I thought of an Enlightened teacher whose birthday we were celebrating. I smiled and felt pretty darn lucky to be in New York studying with another Enlightened teacher in this life.

Throughout this whole episode, I realized that circumstances do not have to dictate whether one is happy or frustrated. Throughout the evening, I steadfastly refused to give into judgment. When I found myself becoming self-indulgent, I immediately started doing some activity that took my mind off my circumstances. By not judging, I held tight control over my emotions.

I remembered what I had taught my students years before that while emotions add color and definition to our experience of life; they are like wild horses in that they must be tamed and controlled if we want to be in charge of our life.

If you enter a corral filled with nervous and excited wild horses, they will try to bite, kick or even kill you. These horses, like your emotions, must be controlled. There is no need to get rid of them. They are valuable. Once they have been tamed and brought under control, they can become a powerful, constructive force in your life.

Jumpy

I had a large apartment in Mount Kisco, New York, that I shared with my son Lonnie. During this time I met a most strange, yet wonderful person, Chaz.

Chaz was a Rama student, and like so many gifted people, he had a somewhat eccentric side. Whenever the subject of rats came up, Chaz would begin an excited dissertation on how misunderstood they were, and what great pets they made. He would speak in disgust at the thought of hamsters.

"Hamsters are so stupid that they could never be good pets. They do not even have enough intelligence to recognize their owners! Rats, on the other hand, are extremely intelligent and loving pets. Why, in India there are temples dedicated to rats! They are thought to be holy expressions of God!" he would exclaim.

When I first met Chaz, he had over fifty rats. He loved his pets. Each one had a name, usually a spiritual name. Sometimes he named them after personality traits or physical abilities.

Of all the rats that Chaz had, Jumpy was his favorite.

One evening Chaz approached me during a break at a meditation. I had casually known him for over a year and I always enjoyed talking with him. He was particularly bright.

"Tony, I need a place to stay for a short while. The lease is up on my current apartment and I haven't been able to locate a suitable place yet."

I liked him but I knew that I could not have all those rats and their cages in my place.

"Chaz, I am willing to let you come and stay with Lonnie and me, but I cannot have a whole menagerie in my building, a cat or small dog perhaps, but not a zoo."

He said he understood.

Two nights later, he approached me again.

"I am desperate. As much as I hate to do it, I will find a home for my little friends, if your offer is still good."

"Sure," I said, "Lonnie and I will make room for you right away."

Over the next few days, Chaz became a supreme salesperson for rats. Rama students were high-pressured into taking a rat home as a pet. It was great watching him overcome all objections as to why they would not be able to have a rat. Chaz would even provide the cage and be a free twenty-four hour consultant on the care and upkeep of these animals. He was highly successful!

As the day arrived for him to move in with Lonnie and me, Chaz pitched his very last rat sale, on me!

"I simply cannot bear to give up Jumpy," he said.

I looked at him. It might have been the look in his eyes that told me of the great sacrifice he had just made and that this pet meant more to him than I could ever fathom. After the way he had found homes for all of the rest of his pets, I felt that I too, could do my share. I relented and gave in.

It came to pass that Chaz and Jumpy became a part of Lonnie's life and mine.

I must say that at first I was apprehensive about having a pet rat in the apartment. However, it did not take long for Jumpy to win my heart.

Jumpy was an extraordinary animal. It took some getting used to, watching Chaz and Jumpy together. Each day Chaz would come home from work, and pick Jumpy out of her cage and stroke and kiss and pet this strange looking animal. He would even open his mouth and stick Jumpy's head inside. They both seem to enjoy this strange ritual. He clearly loved Jumpy.

Chaz would sit Jumpy on the table a feed her from his plate. She had impeccable manners. She would watch him in complete adoration as he worked on the PC. She would sometimes climb up his arm, and sit on his shoulder and watch the screen. Occasionally, she would gently lick his ear. It became clear that Jumpy looked at Chaz not as just this great big friend; she considered him her god.

It was a cold Wednesday evening when I arrived at the apartment. I wandered up the stairs, feeling tired. The train ride from Manhattan had not been very restful and I had put in a hard day's work.

The apartment was dark except for a single light over the kitchen table. Chaz was hunched over the table looking at something.

"Hi Chaz! How's it going?" I exclaimed.

Chaz just sat there. He then looked up at me and I knew something was drastically wrong.

"Jumpy," he choked out.

I walked over to the table and there was Jumpy, or rather, it was her body.

"Jumpy got out of her cage and wandered into the apartment upstairs. They did not know she was a pet. They thought that she was just a huge rat. It was only after they killed her with a butcher knife that they started questioning why she did not try to run away. They didn't know!" he sobbed.

I placed my hand on his shoulder and we shed a few quiet tears together. I could only be with my friend during this time. My estimation of him grew even more as I saw that he did not hold any hard feelings against the ones who murdered his pet. He understood and forgave. Still he mourned. After a while of grieving, I wiped away a tear and said, "Chaz, we have to start considering what to do with the body."

Chaz let out a big sigh and said that he just could not bear to do anything until this weekend.

We wrapped up Jumpy in some tin foil and placed her in the freezer compartment of the refrigerator. This became a temporary morgue for our friend until the weekend.

The next morning as I rode the Metro North train into Manhattan, I thought about Jumpy and Chaz. I wished that there was something I could do or say that would help Chaz through this difficult time. For the life of me, I could not come up with anything.

As I exited Grand Central Station, Steve came up and greeted me. Steve was another Rama student who lived in the City.

"Fancy meeting you here!" he said. "I usually don't walk this way but today I wanted to do things differently. By the way, how is Chaz?"

Before I could answer him and tell him about Jumpy he said, "I had a Rama dream last night! It was the strangest thing. In the dream I was sitting in my apartment and the door creaked open a bit and in walked Jumpy! I wondered how Jumpy had gotten out of her cage and had found her way into Manhattan to visit me. Just as I was about to get up and get her, Rama entered the door. He looked down and saw Jumpy and his expression was like that of someone who just found a lost object. He bent over and Jumpy leaped into his hands. Rama stroked the animal, then looked at me, smiled and waved good-bye. It was an incredible feeling!"

The look on my face must have been something. I felt as though my mouth had dropped a foot! I then told Steve about Jumpy's sudden demise and we talked briefly about Chaz. Finally, Steve said he had to run or be late for work.

"Be sure to tell Chaz about my dream!" he said as he turned to walk away.

"You can bet on it!" I exclaimed.

As I headed out for my job, my heart was singing! Now I had something that would provide comfort for Chaz.

How lucky I was to have a teacher who cared so much, if he cared that way about our pets, how much more for us!

Chapter Nine – Transition Time

The Initiation

Curiosity and apprehension gripped me. This was a special night. Rama said that this night he was going to initiate us as monks of his lineage. This was, to me, the most important graduation I had ever attended.

All of the students had arrived dressed in their finest attire. I gazed around the huge meeting hall. The room was beautifully decorated and had the most beautiful Tankas [3] I had ever seen. There were beautiful balloons and flowers. I was overwhelmed at the beauty of the room. No expense had been spared.

Rama sat down and talked about how, this evening, the Dharma had finally won out for good. He stated that we would be able to continue to shine the light no matter what happened to him. This was a graduation for all of us.

Throughout the talk, the room was filled with a blinding golden white haze that distorted the walls. The various Tankas seemed to come to life and the veil between worlds was thin and at times completely transparent. My spine was locked into a rigid posture and waves of powerful energy surged up my spine.

Rama then had us form a line and come forward for our empowerment.

Finally, there I was standing in front of him. He stands about six foot three, but on this night, he seemed much larger. I closed my eyes and he put his ring and middle finger on center of my forehead in an area known as the third eye. He pressed a little harder on the left side of my forehead and the strangest thing

---

[3] While regarded by some as colorful wall hangings, to Buddhists, these Tibetan religious paintings offer a beauty, believed to be a manifestation of the divine, and are thus visually stimulating.

happened. I felt the energy flow down to my feet and fill up the left side of my body with what seemed to be golden oil. When the energy reached the top of my head, he pressed harder with the finger on the right side of my forehead. Once again, I had the sensation of golden oil flowing down to my feet and filling up that side of my body. The second that the energy reached the top of my head, he removed his hand from my forehead. Then he said, "Good, move to the side."

I do not know how I managed to move at all. However, I must have. In fact, I do not remember much of anything for the next couple of hours. I was definitely in a state of extended awareness.

Later, as I drove back to Mount Kisco, it really hit me. I was now a monk! It felt good! I realized at that time that this was not the first time I had been initiated as a monk. Memories of Tibetan temples and monasteries flooded my mind.

Being a monk was a conscious decision to follow the Dharma [4] for the rest of my life! I was thrilled to have once again taken this commitment, especially with this teacher! I walked on clouds for days!

The Dinner

As I entered the Waldorf Astoria in Manhattan, I was overcome with excitement! What an incredible experience! Everything seemed to have a glow and clarity, much like nature after a rain.

Once inside, I looked around and took in the elegance and beauty of this famous hotel. In the lobby, I saw some familiar faces of people whom I had come to know over the years. I smiled and said hello to those who were within speaking distance,

---

[4] Dharma is the central concept that is used in order to describe the "higher truth" or ultimate reality and purpose of the universe.

but mostly we were keeping our energy tightly focused on the evening as we headed towards the large banquet hall.

Every one of my friends seemed to shine, or rather, exude a light that was clearly apparent, especially to me. All of them were dressed in their finest attire. As this became apparent, I shifted somewhat uncomfortably in my old Tuxedo. I had purchased this suit many years ago, and I knew that it was old and outdated. Compared to them, I felt pretty sloppy. I just did not feel that I was dressed properly. Everyone else was so perfect. It made me wish that I had taken the time to rent a nice Tuxedo. However, I soon realized that the uneasiness I was feeling was not coming from the old suit I was wearing: it was something else. I could not place my finger on why.

I reasoned that perhaps this edgy feeling could be traced back to the fact that I was about to have my first meeting with my spiritual teacher in over four months. I had taken some time off to reorganize my life, and I was overjoyed when I received the invitation to see him again.

Rama loved to hold his meetings in beautiful settings. The amazing dinner this evening was just something he threw in as a nice touch. I always found it amazing how he was able to do all that he did. It was clear to me that the small amount that each of us had paid for this event would not come close to the cost. Rama had made many gestures towards us like this over the years.

Once inside the banquet hall, I found myself immersed in a charged energy that I had come to know so well. This spiritual energy was present whenever I sat with Rama. It felt like some sort of spiritual microwave energy. My spine tingled and my awareness immediately shifted into a heightened state.

I took a moment scanning the room trying to see the "right" chair. There it was. It was three tables back and toward the center. I smiled as I recalled how I had always tried to let the room itself show me where to sit. The chair glowed. I sat down and smiled at those at the table.

I closed my eyes and listened to the music of Zazen. [5] As I listened, the music lifted my spirit and just carried me away. I observed my awareness increase as my thoughts stopped. Soon, I was dissolving into the charged energetic field where there was nothing but golden and white light.

Later the energy shifted and I became aware of my body. Once again, I felt like I had come back home in this amazing spiritual energy, yet strangely I still felt as though I was just visiting. However, the enlightened energy continued to flow through my whole being. It felt wonderful!

As I quietly sat waiting for Rama to enter the room, I let my mind drift back over the years I had spent with my teacher. Suddenly, with in a few short seconds, a series of memories flooded my mind – so many amazing experiences!

Where did it all start?

I knew the journey I shared with Rama started long before this life.

But in this life, I believe it all started with Mickey... [6]

Slowly the memories of the past seemed to distill into the present moment. It was clear that from the beginning with Mickey, and on through my recent initiation in New York, all those years, all that light, all of the transformation and shifts in attention and awareness, that Rama had been the Enlightened Teacher that had guided me on the Fast Path... What an amazing journey!

---

[5] Zazen is a music group that was started by Rama. The music of Zazen provides a perfect atmosphere for meditation. For more details, please visit their website: www.Zazen.com.

[6] The memories that went through my mind during that moment became the stories I have related in this book. I have written these stories as an act of recapitulation with the intent of sharing some of the light, energy, and insights I gained during those years.

As I opened my eyes and gazed around the large banquet hall of the Waldorf Astoria, I perceived that everything was both familiar and yet it still had newness to it. There I was, once again sitting at one of the great hotels in the world, waiting for my teacher. So much had happened during my association with Rama over the years. All of the memories were overwhelming me. So much of my life had been absorbed in the amazing adventure I had with Rama. My very soul was full of love and gratitude.

As this feeling of love and appreciation filled me, I knew Rama was about to enter into the room. As usual, I felt his presence even before he entered the room. The room was filled with golden light and energy in a powerful way. He would be standing in front of us in just a few minutes.

I had not seen Rama for a number of months. It had come as quite a surprise when I heard that he was allowing all of his former students to attend another dinner with him. I looked around and saw several other students who had also not attended in a while. Rama had invited all of us to attend a dinner with his current students.

During the entire time I lived in New York, Rama had allowed me to attend a number of meetings even though I had no money. After about a year, I no longer felt that I could do this. The result was that I had not attended any student meetings in about six months. I began to feel like the rest of the students had slowly left me behind.

For over a year and a half, I had endured a severe personal loss and it had affected me deeply. My girlfriend, Brenda, had suffered a nervous breakdown and disappeared leaving only a weird diary behind. This loss, and my frantic searching for her, had really affected me in a most unhealthy way. When she disappeared, I was devastated.

Rama had made himself available to me several times during this horrible period in a most supporting way. His advice and support of me and his sincere wish to find and help Brenda was stated over and over again. I cannot begin to convey how much his love and support helped me during this ordeal. Now the turmoil and anguish of this loss had finally settled down to a mostly manageable level. I was now functioning again and had the best job of my life. My stream of consciousness was interrupted when Rama walked through the room.

Rama climbed up the stairs on the stage and sat down and he started to meditate as the room turned gold. It always amazed me how he could meditate so powerfully. I really loved him. He talked for a while and, quite honestly, I do not recall too much of what he said. I was dissolving into light!

Rama showed the software products that many of his students had created on a large screen. They were beautiful and had this incredible energy.

Finally, Rama laid out the terms of how we could return as students. They were very high. So high, in fact, it was quite apparent that I would not be able to make the leap at that time. My six months had caused me to fall back and now it seemed impossible to catch up. Many times since I had come to New York, I had attended meetings without any money. I had never been turned away. I knew that I could have probably continued that pattern, but now it just did not seem right.

I listened and observed as Rama continued to talk about his plans and the direction they were going. As he continued to talk, I knew in my heart that this was my time to say good-bye.

It was not the tuition or the lifestyle. It had nothing to do with my situation with Brenda. It was simply time for me to leave the nest and fly on my own.

This saddened and excited me at the same time. I spent the rest of the evening focusing on Rama and the light that came through him. I focused on him as he spoke. I watched the room shift. I wanted to watch him fly just one more time, before I spread my own wings.

Nobody can fly like Rama!

Looking Back

The stories in this book cannot come close to relating how it really was. Rama has the ability to focus his attention on anything and explore it fully.

There were times when he would lead us into the exploration of the various traditional pathways to Enlightenment. Each major pathway was examined and experienced by everyone through our association with him. It really did not seem to matter whether it was Yoga, Zen, Tibetan Mysticism, the teachings of Don Juan as related by Carlos Castaneda, or computer science, Rama became the master of whatever he focused on and he had the awesome ability to take us with him. It was quite a wild ride that caused each one of us to draw deep from within and become extremely flexible in our approach to life.

Throughout it all, Rama gave of himself in ways that are hard to imagine. Some of his students were stubborn, cantankerous and sometimes downright angry as he pushed, coaxed and even drove us into Enlightenment. I never once questioned his love and concern for us. I knew, first hand, of his generosity and compassion. He was, however, a very tough teacher. Looking back, I can fully understand and appreciate his methods.

In the beginning, I had romantic ideas about being a part of a wonderful spiritual community comprised of loving, supportive, peaceful individuals. This simplistic dream did not last long in the reality of Enlightenment. Rama's alchemical vessel of spiritual transformation was an incredibly fast path that at times seemed very volatile.

Each one of us interfaced with this intense energy, drew it through our structures of life, and created our own reality of just who Rama was, as well as the nature of the Enlightenment process. As this hot wind of Dharma blasted through us, we had to let go of our old selves and become the Light, or struggle to reconcile the Light of Eternity with our limited views. This process caused us to constantly change and redefine ourselves.

Because the structures of our beings varied from one to the other, we each saw Rama and this whole experience completely differently. I am convinced that none of us ever really came close to the expansive awareness, knowledge, and extraordinary fullness that is Rama.

I suppose that the same could be said of our view of life or of each other. As Rama said, "Everyone and everything in life is your teacher. Don't trash your teacher."

I have tried to approach all of life as my teacher. As a result, I have reviewed the memories of my life. I chose to take on the awesome task of removing the emotionally charged judgments that have been restricting my seeing. I will continue this process for the rest of my life or until I obtain an unobstructed view of Eternity interplaying with itself in perfection and harmony.

Thanks to Rama, I am able to see this perfect interplay in ways that had eluded me up until our association.

Epilogue

As I look back on my time with Rama, I am filled with wonder and awe. It has been several years since I last studied with Rama as a formal student. I owe him a great debt of gratitude for the great many gifts he has given me. In my own way, I have attempted to return this gesture to Life by sharing this knowledge and awareness with others during the various seminars that I conduct and through my writing.

Words cannot express how this association with Rama has inspired, propelled, and empowered me on this wonderful, adventurous journey, which is now my life.

Thanks, Rama! You awakened me!

Tony

Acknowledgement

Rama - Dr. Frederick Lenz (1950-1998) was a warm and candid Buddhist teacher. He was well known for his best-selling books: *Surfing the Himalayas, Snowboarding to Nirvana, Lifetimes: True Accounts of Reincarnation,* and others.

He developed a form of meditation that emphasizes the importance of focus and concentration to strengthen and clarify the mind. This type of mediation is called Chakra Meditation. It is an adaptation of Tibetan Vajrayana Buddhism, Kundalini Yoga, and Original Zen.

In addition, Rama in collaboration with the music group Zazen, co-wrote and produced 14 musical albums including; *Canyons of Light, Enlightenment, Cayman Blue, and Samadhi.* All of the albums featured music geared towards facilitating the practice of meditation.

After 28 years of teaching, Rama inspired and motivated more than half a million students in the United States and Europe. He was an exciting meditation teacher and an incredible being of light who was able to lead his students into higher states of mind and well-being.

For more information, please visit the following websites: www.fredericklenz.com and www.fredericklenzfoundation.org.

About Mystic-Buddha

With the publication of this, our first book, Mystic-Buddha Publishing House embarks in a journey of discovery. We are looking for new authors who want to write books about Rama – Dr. Frederick Lenz, in a positive light. In addition, we are also looking for people to write great books about meditation, self-discovery, Buddhism in America, and other inspirational topics.

Mission Statement

Our Mission is to disseminate inspiration and wisdom. Mystic-Buddha serves as an open forum for our authors to share their experiences and passion for meditation and self-discovery. Our intent is to serve and benefit all sentient beings by providing stories that inspire and bring knowledge and wisdom into life.

Submissions

We are currently accepting proposals for books (fiction and non-fiction), audio books, and other multimedia projects. For more details, please visit our website: www.Mystic–Buddha.com.

Mystic-Buddha, LLC

Unlike other publishing companies, Mystic-Buddha will not charge its authors for publishing or submitting their works for evaluation. Mystic-Buddha operates as a traditional publishing house. Mystic-Buddha is a registered Limited Liability Company.

CPSIA information can be obtained
at www.ICGtesting.com
Printed in the USA
BVHW040656301020
592196BV00026B/313